Clean Ea

Eat Better, Heal Your Gut, Lose Weight, Boost Your Metabolism

The Ultimate Quick Start Guide with 15-minute recipes to lose up to 15 pounds in 15 days

Table of Contents

Free Gift

As Promised Here Is Your Guide To Managing Stress: Discover The Simple Solutions to Live A Stress Free Life.

<u>GET YOUR COPY HERE</u>

LEARN HOW TO MANAGE YOUR STRESS

Stress can take a huge chunk of your time, energy, and health. Not only your personal relationships suffer, but so as your career and total wellness. Are you struggling from stress? This book explains the true definition of stress, the symptoms and the right way to cure it. Moreover, the book gives tactical strategies to decrease your stress and increase living a happier and healthier life.

>> Download "Stress Management" For FREE<<

Introduction

What have you eaten so far today? As you name the dishes, could you re-create them from scratch right in your kitchen? Could you name all of the ingredients in each dish you ate?

You can't go on to a farmer's field or into his barn and collect most of the food you probably ate today. You can't go there and pick fresh Pop Tarts or white toast off the plant. There are no power bar trees, nor any energy drinks available from the fruit trees in his orchard. There is no instant gravy mix on any bush in his field. There is no instant coffee or synthetic coffee creamer in his barn anywhere near the cows.

I am here to talk to you about real food versus pseudo-food. To talk to you about your choices and the control you have over the food you eat. When you have control over the food you eat, you have tremendous control over your body's health and vitality. Look around you. How many people have true glowing health and vigorous vitality (whatever their age)? Maybe they are making different food choices from you...

Real food is your friend – the best friend your gut and body ever had! Toxins are your enemy – the worst enemy your gut and body could ever harbor within. Eating real food helps flush out those toxins. Flushing out the toxins creates health and ensures lean wellness.

All of us already know what real food is versus denatured foodstuffs. There is enough information out there today that we should be ashamed not to find it – and heed its facts:

- what *real food* is and the *benefits* of eating it
- food-based *allergies* and food-perpetuated *illness*
- the drawbacks to your body, wellness, and health of eating all the *un-food*

Stop ignoring and avoiding what you already know! We simply must start (and continue) to choose what we'll call "clean" or real food and dump all the fake-food substances, the un-food, that we have gotten into the habit of consuming.

In the United States, huge agro-food businesses have been able to produce enormous amounts of very *cheap* food for us. It is not always, however, identifiable as food, because it is no longer whole or raw once it has made its way to us. Many physicians have started to call these other types of products "food-like substances." Sound unappetizing? It should!

This history of cheap food-like substances leads individuals moving into a clean food regimen to complain about the "high cost" of clean eating. Just keep in mind that in many, many parts of the world, whole families are spending **80% of their entire cash income** on clean food and water alone. And they don't eat every day, even with this tremendous expense!

So wake up, and make a decision to take care of yourself through clean eating.

The last section of each chapter is there to help you clean up your act! You'll get a sample of a Clean Eating dish or a recipe to use as an inspiration. Pay attention to the health of your gut and clean up your act ... with real food.

How to do "Clean Eating" can be summarized in _two words_, which we will look at next.

Chapter 1: Add. Eliminate.

The phrase "clean eating" has been around for several decades now, and is sometimes mistreated. Let's define clean eating for our purposes.

Simply stated, clean eating is choosing only foods that are unrefined, unprocessed and identifiable as natural. In order to eat clean, you add unrefined, unprocessed, whole, natural and nutritious types of food to your meals ... and eliminate all the rest.

Add. Eliminate. That is Clean Eating!

The psychology of **adding** and **eliminating** is pretty simple. In my view, your easiest approach is based on starting by *adding* clean food while ignoring the need to eliminate anything. Why? When you add and then begin each meal by eating clean food, you have less room in your stomach (and less craving) for processed or refined foods. *Eliminating the unhealthy stuff, which most of us resist because it means changing our habits, is accomplished for us pretty easily if we are full on the good stuff!*

Add

"Clean" really just means real food. It comes either from Mother Nature in that form (such as a piece of whole fruit or nuts on a tree, or a whole vegetable on a plant in a field or garden, etc.) ... or is sold in as natural a form to its original source as possible (a piece of raw meat or fish from the butcher's counter).

Clean food is (in their original, natural state):

1. Fruit
2. Vegetables
3. Nuts and Seeds
4. Lean Meats
5. Whole grains and beans

6. Herbs and Spices of plant origin

This type of identifiable, unadulterated real food is what you will be **adding** more and more to your meals from now on. At best, you will be starting with those foods in their raw state and cooking/preparing them yourself. That means:

- Buy a piece of raw chicken or fish to broil, grill or bake at home for your dinner
- Purchase your favorite vegetables to steam or boil to eat as a hot side dish
- Purchase your favorite vegetables to eat raw in a big salad to start out a dinner or be your entire lunch
- Buy raw fresh, seasonal fruit from the farmers' market, or grocer's for your breakfast
- Choose high-quality unrefined whole grains (quinoa, amaranth, brown or red rice and wild rice, popcorn, whole-wheat, etc.) to cook from scratch or as the primary ingredient of whole grain bread and crackers

- Eat nuts and seeds (raw or roasted, such as sesame or sunflower seeds, almonds, and walnuts, etc.) and get your dose of *healthy* fats
- Buy dried beans and pulses and *cheaply* make a range of dishes from them

You eat only fresh, living, whole food, in a form as close as possible to what Mother Nature gave us. There is plenty of such food to choose from whether you are a meat / fish eater or are a pure vegetarian. You can do clean eating whether you like to cook a lot, and even if you don't.

Eliminate

When you are eating clean, you ***eliminate*** all processed and refined foods. If you are still not sure what processed or refined foods are:

- If it comes in a bottle, can, package or box of any kind to be stored in the cupboard, fridge or freezer, and it has come to you from a <u>factory</u> rather than a <u>field or farm</u> – it has been processed

- If it has a <u>shelf life</u> longer than a piece of fresh fruit or a raw vegetable, it has likely been processed or refined (obvious exceptions are dried beans and whole grains...)

When you are eating clean, you ***eliminate*** from everything you eat:

1. Extra *sugar* (like spooning artificial sweeteners or granulated sugar into your coffee, tea or into your oatmeal)
2. Extra *salt* from your salt shaker (even sea salt)
3. All *processed* products (condiments such as ketchup, mayonnaise; deli meats; boxed breakfast cereals, etc.)
4. Factory-*refined* foods (such as white flour and everything made from it like bread and pastry; white rice; pasta; foods made from corn flour, etc.)

5. Unhealthy *fat* (as a rule of thumb, any fat which is solid at room temperature, such as in meats, cheeses, and butter)

I feel I must repeat myself somewhat!

Elimination includes avoiding dairy products, alcohols, all caffeinated beverages and sodas of all flavors, and store-bought condiments. Red meat is difficult to digest, so you eliminate this as well. Why? All of those foods are processed, refined, and in the case of dairy/meat products, have solid fats. Processed and refined very likely means that the food-like substance you are considering eating has been pumped up with extra salt, artificial sugar substances, adulterated fats ... and man-made chemicals.

Mother Nature puts the perfect amount and type of sodium (salt) in most of her vegetables. Mother Nature puts the right kind of body-usable sugars (fructose) in her fruit. She also gives us plant foods that have perfect types and amounts of fats in them for our bodies' energetic use (avocados, olives, nuts – all in their whole forms). Not only fat, but protein, minerals, and vitamins (to name the big ones) are contained in ALL plant food in perfect amounts for us.

That *natural* salt, sweetness and fat (and nutrients) is good for us and usable by our bodies thanks to the *fiber* in those natural, whole foods. Eat it whole, and you are doing yourself a healthful favor!

Easier Than You Think

If you are like me and just simply hate to <u>count calories</u>, rest assured that you can do clean eating without counting calories whatsoever. If you have been on diets before and counted calories, you know how inconvenient (not to mention depressing) that can be.

If you have been on diets before that require you to *measure out your <u>carbohydrate, protein, and fat</u>* intake – rest easy! In fact, you don't even need to know what those words mean or which foods they may refer to. You won't have to do that when you stick with the clean eating approach.

And speaking of measuring? Just eat fruit and veg until you're full; don't overeat the other foods on the clean eating list – and you'll be creating greater health!

Follow Your Gut

Clean eating can be inexpensive... or cost a fortune. That depends on you. Don't be surprised to learn that you can do clean eating, and have delicious _cooked_ meals on a small budget. Here's an inexpensive, comfort-food type of dinner that you can throw together in less than 15 minutes. The slow cooker (or the pressure cooker, if you prefer) does all the work.

Easy Veg Chili for a lazy evening entertaining (or vegging out) at home:

Start with raw vegetables and chop them anyway and to any size you like. Frankly, I do it in huge chunks, since I'm throwing all the ingredients in the crockpot / slow cooker. Amounts are approximate and unimportant. Choice of vegetables should be what you love to eat or can afford!

1 medium yellow onion

2 bell peppers, any color

3-5 whole cloves garlic

3-5 whole fresh tomatoes

2-3 cups of seasonal squash – zucchini or yellow squash, butternut squash, etc.

2 carrots

1 cup of corn

2 turnips

2 cups of your favorite type of previously cooked beans – I like chickpeas, kidney beans or black-eyed peas for this chili

1 habanero or other spicy hot pepper of your choice (optional)

1 tablespoon each of ground cumin, paprika, cayenne or other chili pepper, salt to taste

Put everything in the slow cooker with 2 cups of water. Set it on low for 6-8 hours.

This is pretty basic. Not rocket science. But why should _you_ do clean eating? Let's see about that now.

Chapter 2: Why People Choose to Eat Clean

You've had a bit of an introduction to clean eating now, so it's time to get more into the weeds, so to speak, of _why_ you should do so – why you should do clean eating every single day, at every single meal.

This is truly a case of "following your gut." By gut, I mean our entire digestive system and metabolism (which, in a nutshell, is simply our ability to fully use the energy and nutrients from the foods we eat). Many people's gut is sluggish and inefficient. The digestive system has gotten tired of dealing, for years and even decades, with the types of food-like substances you have been eating!

The gut's health dictates the health of the rest of the body! Eating clean helps rebuild and

maintain great health, vitality, and wellness –
by eating clean food that heals your gut.

This is not only important; it is vital to creating
high levels of health and energy. When your gut
is clean, it does its job more efficiently. When it
does its job of digestion and providing the
entire body with 100% usable energy, your
body will start to let go of stored fat. When
your gut is efficient, you need less food ... and
lose weight!

<u>Letting go of stored fat gives you a double
benefit:</u>

- You will lean up and lose weight as that
  stored fat is released.
- Our bodies protect us from toxins by
  surrounding them with <u>fat</u> cells. As we
  eliminate the source of toxins from our
  meals, we don't need those fat cells to do
  that job anymore, right? The fat cells are
  thus released. The toxins are eliminated
  from our bodies as well.

Remember that toxins from food-like substances are what cause illness. Eating clean is vital for getting well and lean again ... or for the first time!

Get ready to feel a higher level of energy from morning till night.

People choose to eat clean for a variety of reasons – yet the first one must be to heal the gut. The gut is all about processing food for energy and support of all body functions.

The beauty of clean eating is that its benefits to you are cumulative:

1. If you are transitioning to clean eating to lose weight, you will naturally *lose your excess weight* over time, as you stick to a clean eating plan
2. If you are transitioning to clean eating on the advice of a medical professional, in order to *reduce or eliminate the*

symptoms of a diagnosis (or the diagnosis itself), you will gradually notice that you achieve this as well, as the toxins leave your body

You are feeding your body fewer toxins – because the food is now clean. You are feeding your body fewer non-nutritious calories – because the food is now whole and natural.

More Benefits and Reasons to Eat Clean

Healthier teeth and gums. Eating starts in the mouth. With your old way of eating, it was your teeth and gums that were your contact point with over-sweetened and overly salty foods. Over time, your teeth and gums will heal from being attacked by the heavy sugar and salt content of the food-like substances you have stopped eating. You'll also actually be using your chewing power more and strengthening your gums – your meals have less pre-chewed processed food and more chewable real food!

Higher levels of energy and sharpness.
This manifests differently from person to
person. It may mean that you notice you are
sleeping better, or for fewer hours yet still feel
refreshed. You may be waking up absolutely
ready to hit the road with enthusiasm. It may
mean that the 4 o'clock slump you used to
suffer from has disappeared. You notice that
your mental acuity and sharpness come back,
as the mental fog from processed and refined
foods dissipates. Your sex drive may improve,
or come back after a long absence. You might
be inspired to get exercise instead of collapsing
on the sofa in the evening.

Lab numbers enter the normal ranges.
Whether blood pressure, blood sugar,
cholesterol, heart rate, urinalysis – your vital
signs and your basic labs will improve. This will
indicate that your body is healing.

Mood and behavior. Children are the first to
experience and show shifts in their typical
moods. When they go from a sugar-rich, highly

processed and refined way of eating to a clean eating program, their highs and lows smooth out. They express less high drama such as tantrums. They listen better. They behave more calmly and respect social conventions more naturally. You as an adult will also experience these shifts – so pay attention for them!

Follow Your Gut

Chicken and Broccoli Stir-un-fry
(All amounts are per person)

1/2 cup boneless chicken (dark or white meat), cut into bite-size chunks
1 cup broccoli florets
1/4-1/2 onion in slices
1 crushed garlic clove – or garlic powder to taste
1/2 inch ginger, grated – or ginger powder to taste – or a tablespoon of chopped fresh hot pepper of your choice

Place a nonstick pan over medium heat and toss in the chicken and onions – no oil or fat, please! When thoroughly cooked, add 3 tablespoons of water to the pan and stir in the broccoli and remaining ingredients. Cover the pan for three minutes, stirring once every minute. If you prefer your broccoli softer, cook for an additional minute or two. Before serving, add 1 tablespoon of melted coconut oil and salt to taste.

Alright, I've given you a few clues to what eating clean looks like on a plate. But how limited is this clean eating approach? Let me show you how _un_limited it can be!

Chapter 3: What You Get to Eat

Is this just another diet? Yes. No.

As regards the food we eat these days, common sense is no longer very common. We have come to rely on "food" suppliers, many of which make food that our grandparents would not have recognized as such! Agro-food businesses have denatured Mother Nature's bounty to the point that we no longer see the edible origin of our food – they sell us "food brands" and "food experiences," rather than the food itself. We no longer detect real vegetables, fruit, meat or any real dairy product such as cheese or milk in our foods. That might be because science has outstripped common sense, and we are eating something from the lab, rather than something from the fields and farms. We are eating and feeding ourselves. But we are sick, not thriving. It doesn't take a scientist to figure out why!

- Clean eating is about paying attention again to the *quality and origin of food* that we are putting in our mouth. Is it really food? Is it identifiable? Are all the ingredients in that food actually natural ... or produced in a laboratory? It's easy enough to ask ourselves these questions. We need to read packaging labels in order to get some of the answers. If we don't understand the ingredients on a complex food label, we need to ask ourselves why we agree to eat it! We need to develop, once again, our ability to detect real food and reject all the fake stuff.

- Clean eating is about having a variety of food groups at every meal – or as close as you can get to that balance. At a *minimum* for your breakfast, you eat raw fruit (no skipping it or settling for a pot of tea only). At a *minimum* for your lunch and dinner meals, you will have either a vegetable plus a whole grain OR a vegetable and a small piece of meat or fish.

- Clean eating is about NOT overeating any one food or any one meal. Remember, there is another meal right around the corner... in spite of what your mind or your taste buds might try to say to the contrary!

Here is how to choose clean food. Remember our ADD / ELIMINATE rules from the first chapter, which tell us to begin by:

1. adding clean food to each meal
2. eating that clean food first, at each meal
3. eating less and less of the pseudo-food, until we are eating no more of it

Breakfast, Lunch, and Dinner

Focus on fruit! Clean food for breakfast can include

- whole, raw fresh fruit – or fruit blended as a smoothie
- whole, unrefined grain (like quinoa or steel-cut oatmeal or brown rice), eaten as cereal
- raw or roasted nuts or seeds – on their own, or mixed with the fruit, the smoothie or your cereal
- almond or rice milk, no added sweeteners
- (green) tea or black coffee if you must, no added stuff!

Focus on vegetables! Clean food for lunch or dinner can include

- more whole, raw, juicy fresh fruit as a starter
- a bowl of one or more types of steamed vegetables, eaten hot or cold <u>AND</u>
- a bowl of one or more types of raw vegetables, eaten as a salad – or a blend of fruit (apples, raisins) and vegetables (leafy greens, cucumber, celery, etc.) as a raw salad
- A grilled piece of chicken / piece of fish <u>OR</u>
- A hot side dish of whole grain (quinoa, wild rice, etc.)

Notice how we *double up on vegetables* (cooked plus raw at both lunch and dinner)? Notice how we *alternate between grains and animal protein*? Both strategies speed up the cleansing of your intestine – and please remember that is **your secret** to greater health and leanness!

Why? Vegetables are high in both fiber and water, and easily clean your gut at every meal. More gut-cleansing action is better for detoxification. NOT eating grains and meat/fish together in the same meal also allows your digestive system to do a more complete, quicker digestion and assimilation of energy – Natural Hygienists have known this for a couple of centuries! Each food group uses a different combination of digestive enzymes, so keeping your tummy overloaded with both food groups at once makes for sluggish digestion. That's the theory, anyway, and most people anecdotally confirm that they feel better and lighter after meals when they follow this food-combining rule ... and load up on low-calorie vegetables twice a meal, twice a day, too.

Reality Check Exercise: Go to the market and count the number of different vegetables you could eat raw, and then the number you could probably only eat cooked. Make a note. Now count the number of different fruit available and make a note.

And you dare try to tell me there's nothing to eat on this plan?!

Follow Your Gut

Chopped Raw Salad

The guideline on this recipe is: Eat what you love. Look at the vegetables in the produce department of your grocer's. Choose vegetables you really like to eat raw, making sure you have at least four colors.

Examples –

carrots

fresh basil leaves

2 kinds of lettuce

celery

green onions

cherry or pear tomatoes

Peel the carrots and wash everything up. Rough chop all the vegetables (except the cherry tomatoes) and toss them in the food processor. Pulse the vegetables until they are the size of the cherry tomatoes. Pour the vegetables out into a salad bowl and top it with the tomatoes.

Clean Salad Dressing

1-2 ripe avocados

1-3 juicy oranges – alternatively, use 2 lemons or limes

pepper and salt to taste

Put the avocado meat and the whole peeled citrus fruit in the blender together with a couple of shakes of black pepper and salt. If it is too thick for salad dressing – slowly add a tablespoon of water at a time. Pour this over your chopped salad and stir well. It is *real food, so no need to limit how much you use!*

Alternatively, use 4-5 frizzy kale leaves (no stems) instead of avocado. This was a vegetable farmer's recommendation to me!

Well, the real food choices are vast. But what chance do you have of losing weight, or (more importantly) healing your body through clean eating? That's next!

Chapter 4: More on Detoxing and Leaning Up

If a physician has directed you to this new pattern of eating, it is probably because a diagnosis requires you to **_detoxify_** your body so that it can heal more quickly. Perhaps your actual diagnosis is that you are overweight and you need to lighten up with the help of better food choices.

Food Identification

First, ask yourself if you are looking at real food or pseudo-food! Can you name this food that you are adding to your meal? How many ingredients does it have? Can you pronounce them? Do they grow in nature? Food identification is simply an exercise in finding real food that is Mother Nature's own so that you can reject the rest!

Eliminations

With our Add/Eliminate rule, you are already making clean food choices and consuming these foods at the beginning of each meal.

That is the start for all clean eating transitions – fill your plate and your tummy with the good stuff first. Will you still be tempted by pseudo-food? Undoubtedly! But it's not a reason to beat yourself up. Take responsibility for how you will be permanently eliminating the "unclean" food. You can personalize things by eliminating one food or food group at a time, one week after the other, until you are there. Or by deciding to go cold turkey and tossing out all of the food-like substances that you have in your home, or that you purchase outside the home.

Allergies and Toxicities – Test Yourself

The real reason why most people benefit from clean eating is that so many foods (real or

pseudo) are individually toxic to them.
Everyone has heard of food allergies. But not
everyone realizes they may be subject to one or
more of them! By eliminating the top gut-and-
health irritating food groups for three full
weeks – and doing so one group at a time – you
can perform a Do-It-Yourself allergy and
toxicity test. If you find after three weeks that
some unwanted symptoms have disappeared
right along with that food group, this is your
clue to stop eating those foods!

If you are bloated, have skin irritations, feel
unwell after meals or crave any specific type of
food, have a foggy brain all or part of the day,
have mood swings – perform a Do-It-Yourself
allergy and toxicity test!

- Many people have discovered gluten
  intolerance in this way
- Others have discovered allergy to certain kind
  of nuts (cashews and peanuts are the most
  common)
- Others are lactose intolerant

- One young child I met had no tolerance for sugar – she fell asleep immediately on consuming *any type* of commercial sugar! Talk about a weird reaction to food...

Maybe none of this applies to you. But how will you know unless you eliminate each food group for three weeks? If you are doing clean eating to improve your health, you owe it to yourself to perform this Do-It-Yourself allergy and toxicity food test.

I repeat – you eliminate these for 3 full weeks. The top toxic and allergy-prone food groups that you are eliminating for your Do-It-Yourself allergy and toxicity food test can include (in case you still had any doubts):

- **Milk/Dairy** and all its related products. Eliminate cow's and goat's milk – basically milk from any animal. You have to get creative here because milk is found in many products besides just that gallon of liquid milk! You are also, therefore eliminating cheese, yogurt, butter, cream of all kinds, cream cheese, buttermilk and most pastries and desserts (because they contain butter or milk products) and milk/cream-containing sauces and gravies made on your stovetop, etc.

- **Eggs** and all products containing eggs in any form. This will include egg whites, yolks dried eggs, reconstituted eggs and anything called albumin. Keep in mind the number of products containing eggs can include pastries and desserts, condiments, egg noodles and hot sauces of all kinds.

- **Nuts** such as peanuts, pecans, walnuts, cashews, etc. – and all products containing these. Keep in mind that bottled oils are made from such nuts, so you will not be using bottled oils of any kind, just to be sure. And like milk and eggs, you will not be consuming any prepared products containing, or risking to contain, nuts.

- **Wheat**, and all products containing them. This includes even the whole wheat and organic versions for this test. Buying food becomes very easy when you eliminate wheat from your diet – no more baked goods, breads, noodles or pastas, crackers and semolina, boxed cereals or protein/energy bars. Gluten (an allergen that gets a lot of media coverage) is contained in almost all grains from wheat itself (including spelt, kamut, durum, bulgur, semolina, couscous grain), barley, rye, triticale, and oats. The good news is that you *can eat brown rice, wild rice, amaranth and quinoa* during this test – and they are all delicious!

- **Caffeine**. Many Europeans and Americans will revolt against this elimination. How can we possibly start our day without the kick of caffeine? The truth of the matter is, our guts do not care very much for the hard acidity of caffeine from coffee and black teas, from energy drinks and sodas. And remember we are doing this elimination diet to heal our gut! So, during a three-week elimination period, prepare to go without caffeine in any form. Drink lots of water whenever the symptoms hit you; it will make the withdrawal symptoms dissipate more quickly.

- **Added Sugars.** You can Google a New Zealand study about added sugars and mental health in children. The study concluded that almost all our children were diagnosed incorrectly with mental health disorders – when it was their sugary diet that was the culprit. So in this elimination phase, you will be identifying sugar by all the names that the food industry gives it, and avoiding it conscientiously. This is not just about added sugar that you used to spoon into your iced tea or coffee or onto your oatmeal! This is about the hidden sugar in processed foods. Be aware that there are dozens of names for commercial products that sweeten our foods – and not all of them come from Mother Nature. See this website to further educate and inform yourself, so that when you read a label, you can quickly identify the sweeteners and sugars that have been added to the food: https://www.sugar.org/all-about-sugar/the-other-26-sweeteners/.

- **Corn**. Corn is as pervasive in our processed foods as is wheat. It is also highly refined. Why do you need to eliminate this in particular? American corn has been genetically modified (GMO), and many, many people have an unknown intolerance to it. Their gut just doesn't like it! From high fructose *corn* syrup in our canned tomatoes to our favorite corn tortilla chips and snack foods – you're going to need to read lots and lots of labels because corn is virtually in all processed foods. Do you see the beauty now of simply eliminating processed foods from your Clean Eating diet? It makes everything super easy when there are no processed foods involved – no more label-reading! However, to discover your allergies, doing a three-week elimination of all corn and corn products is highly educational for you – so do it!

- **Alcohol.** We all know what this is. Beer is alcohol, as is wine. This includes all the nonalcoholic mixer beverages, powders and any ingredients you add to hard liquor to make a drink. Cut it out. Zero booze for 3 weeks. Notice the difference.

Words to the Wise: If you have been paying attention, you realize that most of the food groups I have listed above do not belong to any kind of clean eating program in the first place! As you transition into full time, 100% clean eating, you can experiment with the above eliminations. I believe it is the best way for you to discover not only how you have been mistreating your gut and health with your food choices – but how easy it is to go without them forever.

Additions

What do you **add more of** after these eliminations? The good stuff! Clean stuff! The real food!

Remember: Our bodies hold onto toxins by wrapping them up in fat cells. That keeps the toxins out of our bloodstream and organs. As you eat fewer toxins (because you have been eliminating them from your diet), your body needs fewer fat cells. Letting go of the toxins goes hand-in-hand with letting go of the fat. The weight melts off your body, and the toxins are eliminated through the bowels, urine and sweat.

For detoxification purposes – but also for leaning up, here is what you *add more* of:

- More green and other vegetables of all kinds, raw and fresh. Go for lots and lots of variety and colors! Vegetables are by definition low in calories (except olives, nuts, and avocados) – so eat up as much as you want at lunch and dinner!
- As a meat eater or fish eater, you will choose organic, range fed or wild caught. Do not overeat this type of food!
- You can add freshly (not bottled) centrifuged fruit and/or vegetable juices. Vegetable juice is low in calories, detoxifying and nutritious! You will prefer however to drink smoothies because of the fiber they retain, on the condition that the only ingredients are raw fruit and/or vegetables – no protein or nutritional powders, nothing from a

can, no added sweeteners. Blended smoothies in the morning and evening add nutrients and natural water to the body to help it flush toxins from your system.

- If you have not been a water drinker, add 4-6 *more* glasses per day to your routine (add some fresh lemon or lime juice to the water, float a piece of real ginger in your glass, or a slice of cucumber).

Follow Your Gut

Seriously consider an all-fruit morning every day. If you have time, or it's winter and cold, or you just feel like a change – try a clean version of a childhood favorite.

Breakfast Bowl

1 cup steel cut oatmeal (not an instant oatmeal!)
1 raw apple, sliced

1 small handful of raisins or chopped dates

cinnamon to taste

a squeeze of lemon juice

Before going to bed, especially if you need to get going quickly in the morning, soak the oatmeal in 1 cup of cold water. Leave it overnight. In the morning, add 1 more cup of water (for a total of 2 cups water to 1 cup oats), and cook the oatmeal on the stovetop on a low to medium heat with the raisins/dates. Serve it up and stir in the apple slices. Sprinkle cinnamon, add a squeeze of lemon juice and eat up. If you like, add a splash of rice or almond milk (unsweetened variety).

For more samples of clean eating meals, read on!

Chapter 5: 15-Minute Meals; 15 pounds; 15 Days

I am putting my disclaimer for this chapter right up front. When you do clean eating, you definitely can prepare a healthful and delicious meal in 15 minutes, and often less.

However, I cannot guarantee that you will lose 15 pounds in 15 days even though almost everyone *does lose weight*. Here is why. I don't know if you're following the clean eating plan – or in plain English, if you're cheating. I don't know how big you are and if you even have 15 pounds to lose. I don't know if you exercise. I don't know if you're even doing clean eating to lose weight! Maybe you're doing it to heal a diagnosis or an allergy, or to let go of some symptoms that have been bothering you.

This said, to lose weight:

- Go heavy on water-rich vegetables, both raw and steamed
- See the section on fruit all morning and do it!

Let's divide the day into three clean meals and see how fast we can prepare them.

Recipes for Whole Meals

If you haven't cooked very much at home, or are prepared to protest that you don't even know how to cook – you'll find that this is quite easy. These are not so much recipes as guidelines for how to put together a whole clean meal in short order. These are just more samples for you of what *clean eating meals* look like. They are raw, cooked, roasted or steamed – and full of variety, color, and flavor to keep you in touch with clean, health-building, energizing living foods!

Breakfast

WEIGHT-LOSS TIP: If you are indeed eating clean in order to lose weight and/or to heal your gut for any reason, most people find that <u>this</u> breakfast is their **number one secret weapon.** It requires you, however, to stick like glue to the formula and to eat clean for the rest of the day as well.

Many, many people in the clean eating community also love this breakfast the most just because it's the fastest, tastiest, most satisfying, sweetest meal of the day.

What is it? It's raw, whole fruit!

No preparation, except washing, is usually necessary. Maybe you'll peel or cut an orange, sure. That's it.

Commit to eating nothing but whole, raw juicy and sweet fruit from the time you wake up until your midday meal, and your body wellness and energy levels will shift within days.

Eat as much as you want without gorging. Go back a couple hours later and eat some more. Morning is fruit time. Don't count calories or pieces of fruit. The combined fiber and natural water content of whole, raw fruit hydrates, flushes, cleans and cleanses your gut (intestines) and thus your entire body at a cellular level. Never, ever underestimate the value of an all-whole-raw-fruit morning!

Go with seasonal fruit. In the summertime, that's berries, apricots; in autumn and early winter it's apples and pears; in full winter it's citrus fruit season. Your goal is to eat it "straight from the tree," for the highest level of nutrition. Going with seasonal fruit is cheaper, too!

EXAMPLE: When I started doing this, I did not foresee the mountain of fruit that I would be eating every morning for the first two weeks! Then my body got used to the pace, the nutrition, and the water content – and now I eat about 4-5 pieces of fruit in the morning and am satisfied and full.

On the go? Pack up some whole fruit. Pack whole apples, pears and bananas. Just pack juicier fruit in lockable baggies – berries of all kinds, peeled citrus fruit slices and so on. Get creative!

WARNING: Fresh squeezed or freshly centrifuged juices are *not* part of this breakfast. The reason? There is no fiber in those juices. Fresh veg and fruit are fiber and nutrient-rich "water." Thus, two things happen in the body after a no-fiber juice (no heavy science here):

1. The natural sugar of the juice spikes your blood glucose levels, meaning that you'll take an energy dive an hour or two later ... and perhaps start craving the wrong kinds of food.

2. Your intestines will not be cleansed and healed because the fruit's fiber is absent.

It's the fiber that does this work, hand in hand with the natural waters of the raw fruit. Please note that this is also true of raw vegetables in your clean eating program.

Eat whole, raw, juicy fruit! Do it for 15 days (and then 15 more and then repeat again) and keep track of how you feel and how your body reacts and adjusts. Yes, you will be on the toilet a lot! You body is quite literally *releasing toxins* through your bowel movements and urine! Go with it; *releasing toxins* is your body's job because that is how it gets and keeps you healthy!

Lunch

In the United States, lunch can be an at-your-desk affair which you eat in three minutes flat or over an hour and a half. It can be a sit-down waiter-served meal with clients, or a grab and go from the local fast food joint that you eat in the park.

A clean lunch can be any of those – as long as the basis for your meal is whole natural food. Here are some examples of lunch for your brown bag days.

EXAMPLE: Homemade chickpea hummus with raw cherry tomatoes, celery sticks, zucchini sticks, wedges of bell pepper, and whole-grain crackers.

Eat as much of any of these ingredients as you like (I tend to go without the crackers). The water and fiber content of the vegetables fill your tummy so that you feel satisfied. Don't overeat, though!

Hummus is extremely fast and easy to make. Buy 1 pound of dry chickpeas (also called garbanzo beans). Soak them in room-temperature water in a large bowl for three hours. Drain and soak them in very hot water for another hour. Drain again then put them in a large pot with some fresh water and boil them until the beans are soft. Put the beans in a food processor along with cloves of garlic, chopped parsley and a whole peeled lemon. Blend until it's very creamy. You can store this hummus for up to a week in the fridge in an airtight container.

VARIATIONS: Play with adding your favorite herbs or spicy spices to this basic recipe. Examples include adding fresh chopped basil or mint leaves, sprinkling it with paprika, black pepper or the spicier cayenne pepper. Mediterranean cooks will also stir in chopped roasted bell peppers or fresh raw hot peppers of any variety they have on hand. If I am eating this lunch at home, I tend to pull out all the raw vegetables I have in the fridge or on the counter at the time, and I dive in!

TIP: Beans are a protein- and fiber-rich food that allow clean eaters to have numerous non-meat and non-fish meals, and still feel satisfied. (Please note that animal products – dairy, meat, and fish – have no fiber.) Clean eaters adapt the hummus recipe to all kinds of cookable beans. I have done this with kidney beans, navy beans, black-eyed peas, lentil beans and others. Very fast. You can prepare it in advance for a whole week. Delicious. Clean.

Dinner

Preparing a clean eating dinner is also quick and simple. Can you spend an hour in the kitchen cooking and following recipes? Yes, you can, if that is what you enjoy. But our philosophy of spending as little time preparing as eating can create some delicious dinners, too!

EXAMPLE: Chopped salad (raw), quinoa and herbs, grilled chicken breast. Yes! I have actually made this meal in 15 minutes.

Chicken breast – start with this. Turn on the broiler, put the chicken breast on a broiler pan after sprinkling both sides with ground pepper and your preference of dried herbs (such as a basil, rosemary, sage blend). Cook it for six minutes on one side and probably five minutes on the other...until cooked through.

Quinoa – while the chicken is broiling, measure 1 cup of dry quinoa and 2 cups of hot water into a saucepan. Cook this just as you do a pot of rice. It will take 12 to 15 minutes.

Chopped salad – see that recipe above.

Serve up the chicken, hot quinoa (which is the highest protein grain, by the way), and a huge portion of your chopped salad. Dive in!

NOTE: My take on clean eating is to avoid fried food or foods cooked in oil or fat. That is why my "stir-un-fry" had no oil... until after the food was cooked. In other words, the coconut oil was raw and simply melted into the food, rather than used to fry it. It was a nutrient and a flavoring (and smells great!) – an ingredient among others. Use your common sense. Keep the amount of heated fats at a minimum if you are clean eating to lose weight and heal!

Follow Your Gut

After eating clean morning, noon and night for seven days, you should be feeling different. Better. Lighter. More energized.

If you are not? It's time to do an elimination cycle with one food group at a time. Ask yourself what the most likely culprit is for you, because frankly? I'm sure you already know! It is very likely that after a meal with wheat which leaves you feeling sluggish – it is the wheat group you need to eliminate now. If after heavy dairy or cheese meals, you don't feel very good or are not digesting – that's the group you eliminate. Use your head! But follow your gut. And in the next chapter, you'll see how to get better organized for clean eating success.

Chapter 6: More Clean Eating Meals

This chapter is all about getting organized for success, including:

1. how much and what kinds of food to keep on hand at home
2. what to do when you eat in a restaurant or when you are traveling or on the go
3. more clean recipes

Foods to Purchase for Home

Here is what a BASIC 100% clean eating shopping list might look like (depending on the season for fruits and vegetables, of course):

Fresh raw fruit

- apples and pears, lemons and oranges and citrus fruit of all kinds, bananas, plums and apricots, mangos and papayas, melons of all kinds, raisins and dates (these are dried, but "clean" choices nonetheless)

Fresh raw vegetables

- tomatoes, three or four varieties of leafy lettuce (green and red leaf, Romaine, spinach), two or three kinds of leafy (kale and broccoli) and head cabbage (white and red cabbage, Savoy cabbage, Chinese cabbage), carrots, asparagus, celery, turnips, potatoes, eggplant, bell peppers, zucchini and summer squash, winter squash (spaghetti squash, butternut squash), fresh herbs (basil, mint, parsley), sun-dried tomatoes
- green herbs like basil or dill, etc.

Raw (or *unsalted* and roasted) nuts and seeds

- almonds, walnuts and pecans, Brazil nuts, sesame and pumpkin seeds, flax and Chia seeds

Whole grains and tubers/roots

- grains to boil as side dishes – brown and red rice, wild rice, quinoa, amaranth, buckwheat, barley
- whole grains baked in breads and crackers, without preservatives or additives – Ezekiel bread, whole grain crackers
- sweet potatoes and yams, turnips and root celery, and (if you must) white or red potatoes
- popping corn

Meat and fish – purchased raw / whole

- skinless turkey/chicken – breast or thighs
- fish such as salmon, tuna

- seafood such as jumbo shrimp or scallops

More for Breakfast

Here is a different take on breakfast from the all-fruit approach.

Drink lemon or lime water upon wake up. Whether you prefer it warm or chilled – drink it! Two glasses are better than one. A pot of light, plain, unsweetened *green* tea comes next (organic is great, but just get the best quality that you can) – unless you prefer to go straight into breakfast. Can you drink black coffee? Up to you, and how badly you want to heal your gut. The consensus is generally to eliminate coffee entirely from your diet and dial back even on green and herbal teas. Do what you can do. If the best you can do is make your sweetened milky coffee into a straight black beverage – do that for a while. If the best you can do is have half a cup instead of the whole pot – definitely do that. Use your head and your common sense.

Whether you move directly into your breakfast or wait a couple of hours, your powerhouse clean breakfast is fruit-plus-green-vegetable based. The easiest way to do this is with a smoothie. Make enough to have two large glasses per person. Each serving can be three bananas (or five apples plus some berries, oranges or other citrus fruit), a handful of spinach leaves, a handful of kale leaves (even with the stems if they are not too thick) or some ordinary parsley. Throw in half a peeled lemon and some filtered water and turn your blender on! Remember – no protein or nutritional powders, no cooked foods, no added sweeteners. Just real, raw, cleansing live food.

If you are doing the fruit-only mornings (previous chapter), adding a fresh green will support that and bring more fiber and different nutrients.

Or, of course, you can sit down to a basket or bowl full of fresh raw fruit that you eat whole. Make sure to eat a variety of fruit, once again. Maybe have a couple of bananas, a couple of seasonal apples or citrus fruit, some berries – whatever is in season, or whatever was cheapest at the time when you were at the market!

Can you eat whole grain bread with your fruit-and-greens breakfast? Yes. But only if wheat, grains and/or gluten are not something you are eliminating in this three-week period.

Same thing with eggs and all dairy. If these are now eliminated for three weeks, you will naturally choose something else for breakfast.

More for Lunch

Most clean eaters I know will stick with a raw vegetable salad for lunch – perked up with a homemade salad dressing, a small handful of nuts or/and slices of one apple. Most people truly feel that it fills them up quite enough, and working people are simply too busy for more anyway.

If they don't go with that salad, they will take leftovers from last night's clean eating dinner. When you are a clean eater, you will learn to get organized and prepare for meals in advance through your shopping list. You also make more of each clean eating dish than you will consume during that meal so that you have leftovers to pack and go the next day.

More for Dinner

Many clean eaters will eat a quick cooked meal in the evening, and as I said, make enough for the next day's leftovers. Dinners may include a vegetable and whole-grain casserole, or a raw vegetable salad with leftover chopped meat or fish or a poached egg or two on top of it, or simply one big bowl of raw vegetable salad accompanied by one big bowl of steamed hot vegetables. Why not start your dinner with a mixed vegetable smoothie? If you have a sweet tooth, you may prefer to start your dinner with a piece of juicy fruit or an all-fruit smoothie. Why not?

Clean Eating Out

Even the fussiest eaters can find _one_ clean eating item on the menu at virtually every restaurant ... except perhaps a few fast food places. It may mean that you don't eat your typical meal or even your preferred one. Just remember that there is always another meal around the corner at home to make it up.

Also keep in mind that if a restaurant you are at with clients or friends has just one clean eating salad (and nothing else) on their entire menu, you are totally free to order two of them, or even three. You can ask for no (processed) dressing on the salad, but lemon slices on the side. You will survive with just a squeeze of lemon in place of salad dressing this one time!

Any restaurant serving grilled chicken or fish in any dish will be more than happy to just serve the chicken all on its own as a side without any gravy or cheese on top of it, even if the restaurant has no other clean eating vegetables to offer.

If you're at a burger joint, and you are on a wheat elimination cycle, order a turkey burger without the bread but with extra salad fixings. Instead of ketchup, have just slices of tomato. After all – it's a restaurant, and whatever they have in the kitchen, they're happy to serve up most any way you ask!

You may find that you are very often only ordering the restaurant's side dishes. And why not? The waiter really doesn't care what you order.

More Recipes to Help You Follow Your Gut

Here are more sample recipes for clean eating that anyone – experienced in the kitchen or not – can whip up with ease, usually in 15 to 30 minutes. Remember to make enough of your favorite meals for leftovers the next day!

Lunch and dinner meals are interchangeable. Remember to *eat fruit on its own*, either before other food or as a mono meal (you will digest it faster and more beneficially). Also, try to *double up on vegetables* by having a raw vegetable dish alongside a cooked vegetable dish in the same meal. You will help your gut and body lean up and clean up that much faster!

Pulled Pork or Stewed Chicken

Choose a pork rump. Select a whole chicken, which the butcher has cut up for you. I like to remove the excess fat from the pork and the skin from the chicken first.

The pork: put the whole piece of raw pork in the slow cooker and cover it with root beer or ginger beer. Set it on low and come back 6-8 hours later. The pork already pulls apart on its own. Separate it from the juices and serve. I personally don't use the juice from this recipe. Pulled pork is great with any kind of raw salad.

The chicken: put the whole chicken or the chicken pieces in a big pot. Cover it with one part red wine and one part water (this may mean 2 cups wine and 2 cups water, for instance). Set the heat on low and walk away for two or three hours, then check it every hour. The chicken should also pull apart on its own when cooked. Lift it out with a slotted spoon and serve. I like to use the wine- and chicken-infused juice from this pot over rice, mashed yams or steamed vegetables. I just ladle it out of the pot and onto my veg. Stewed chicken is wonderful with boiled yams (just peel, slice and boil until soft) and stewed greens.

Stewed Greens

The American South knows all about stewed greens. However, this recipe makes it without fat (no bacon or ham). Every Southern household has its own mix of greens that it prefers. Here's a sample to inspire you.

1 bunch each of washed, rough chopped spinach, kale, collard greens, Swiss chard, mustard greens
1 medium yellow or white onion, sliced
3 tablespoons of crushed fresh garlic or equivalent in garlic powder
1 teaspoon each of paprika and mild curry
Salt and black pepper to taste
3/4 cup homemade soup broth from a prior meal (the wine water from the stewed chicken) or plain water

Just toss it all in a pot and keep stirring on medium heat until the greens have melted. Then cover the pot and put it on lowest heat; let it simmer gently for 30 minutes. Serve it up with the pulled pork and ladle some of the juices over it. I like to squeeze a little lemon juice on it on the plate.

Great Guacamole

Guacamole is basically mashed avocado, dressed up with your choice of seasonings and other vegetables. Avocados give you your daily dose of healthy, usable fat. On the days I eat avocados, I skip meat, nuts, and eggs ... but you use your own common sense.

Here are two variations to inspire you.

2-4 ripe avocados, mashed
½ finely grated carrot
1 finely sliced green onion (use the white bulb and the green stem)
1 stalk grated or finely sliced celery
cayenne pepper and ground cumin to taste
juice of 1 whole lemon or lime

2-4 ripe avocados, mashed

1 large diced fresh tomato, or any cherry
tomatoes, cut in half
2 slices red onion, finely diced
your favorite hot sauce, to taste OR 1 teaspoon
per avocado of finely chopped fresh chili
pepper of your choice
salt to taste

Add some water to thin the avocado
guacamole, and you have yet another avocado-
inspired salad dressing!

Nutty Salad Cream

Since nuts (especially raw) are one of our
healthy fats, and we eat a lot of vegetables –
why not make a salad dressing but with nuts?
My all-time favorite is <u>cashew cream</u>. Soaking
increases digestibility and also allows the nuts
to absorb more water, which is great for your
gut!

1 cup raw cashews, which you have soaked in
plain water for two hours and drained

Freshly ground black pepper to taste
1 tablespoon of nutritional yeast – optional –
(you get this at a health food store – it is not
the stuff you use to make bread!)
3-5 dates, soaked in warm water for 15 minutes
and drained before using (optional, for those
who like a bit of sweet)

Keep in mind that cashews are among the
sweetest nuts you will eat, so try it without
dates first! Throw it all in the blender until it's
smooth. You may have to add a little water to
get the cashews to fully purée. Add water until
you get your preferred salad cream consistency.
You can save this in the fridge for several days.

HINT: if you keep the cashew cream quite
thick, you can use it as a dip for vegetable
sticks. Divine!

Great Grain Casserole

If you like one-dish meals, consider this one.
Here is a basic recipe, which allows countless

variations. The ingredient amounts are per person.

2 cups cooked grain – Brown rice is the classic, and you can try it in the Basmati version for a lighter, nuttier taste
1 small onion, finely sliced
1 cup sliced mushrooms of any type – Portobello bring a nice meaty taste
Italian herbs (thyme, rosemary, sage, basil), salt and pepper to taste
5-6 cloves crushed garlic
2 zucchini or other summer squash, grated

Raw mushrooms and zucchini have a lot of water, which they give off upon cooking. So stir the raw mushrooms and zucchini into your cooked grain, along with the slices of onion and crushed garlic. Your goal is to bake this at 350° (a medium oven) until the mushrooms and zucchini have given up their water. Serve along with a big raw salad.

An alternate version of this baked dish is to substitute sweet potato or yam and a hard winter squash such as butternut squash for the rice. Start with raw potatoes or squash, which you peel and chop into 1-inch cubes. All of the other ingredients can remain the same... or mix it up according to your taste!

Yet another version of this is to use spaghetti squash. You must bake this spaghetti squash first – just cut it in half, scrape the seeds out with a spoon and put it on a baking sheet for an hour in a medium oven (350°). Use a fork to scrape out the softened squash from the husk. It comes out in fibrous strands (hence the name spaghetti). Layer the spaghetti squash with the ingredients in your basic recipe and bake it again until the added raw vegetables give up their water.

Tomato Sauce for All Occasions

This is a slow cooker clean tomato sauce. It is delicious on the aforementioned spaghetti squash! You can also spoon it onto any other grains like quinoa, or into any steamed mixed vegetables that are on your menu, or over your meat/fish of the day. Start with only raw (not canned or frozen) vegetables. I always make the maximum amount my pot will hold, because this sauce never lasts long!

3 pounds of seasonal ripe tomatoes
1 pound grated carrots
1 pound finely sliced cabbage of any type
2-3 large onions of any type, finely sliced
1 entire head of peeled, crushed garlic cloves
1 bunch fresh herbs like dill or cilantro, finely chopped

Layer the vegetables in a slow cooker (a pressure cooker could also be used for this recipe). First the carrots, cabbage on top of that, then the onions, garlic, and herbs, all of the tomatoes. Set the slow cooker for 6 to 8 hours (probably 30 to 40 minutes in a pressure cooker). When cooked, you can simply stir all the ingredients up in the pot and use the sauce with those remaining chunks. Or you can blend the cooked vegetables for a smoother sauce. Use your imagination for when and how to eat this delicious, healthy sauce!

Conclusion

We _need_ to Eat Clean because our current habits are making us sick! We are losing the life and vitality of our bodies – it is draining right out of us. We have appallingly little energy to _live_ our lives. It's because of the pseudo-food, silly! Time to pay better attention to just what sort of food that is.

Our current un-food or food-like substances that the big-food industry produces for us have many downsides. The biggest downside? The food industry has been selling us flavors and brands, rather than the nutrition and healthful calories that our bodies crave! We have bought into that hype. We have let the agro-food business do our thinking for us, and have stopped even trying to identify real food on our plate. Pay attention! Our world is awash with real food. Go get it! You do have control.

Those processed and refined products (it is hard to call them food) are calorie-rich and nutrient-poor. They are deliberately filled with addictive food industry chemicals, flavorings and sweeteners, artificial this and imitation that, which have us mindlessly craving more of that same calorie-rich, nutrient-lacking product. So we do eat more of it. We eat more because our body is looking for the nutrition that it so desperately needs. The body is yelling, "Feed me with real food nutrients!" We pack on the calories. And the extra pounds around our middle. But the nutrients still aren't there.

The processed and refined foods in all sorts of packaging that line the aisles of our grocery stores might not be killing us, but are making our lives miserable by leading to our lack of vitality and energy, poor health, mental fog, mood swings, overweight and other medical diagnoses. Our gut cannot keep up.

It is time to clean up our act. It's time to listen to our gut, which has been suffering for far too long. It cannot do its job on pseudo-food. It needs us to start eating clean, to eat as much fiber-dense and water-logged unrefined and unprocessed foods as we can. The more food we eat in its raw, natural state – raw nuts and seeds, raw fruit and raw vegetables, whole untreated grains and root vegetables, high-quality whole meat and fish – the more nutrition we are feeding our body with each bite.

Clean Eating at its core involves nothing more than common sense, attention to real foods, and a little bit of planning. There aren't many rules:

1. Choose whole, real, fresh unprocessed and unrefined foods from Mother Nature. The variety, colors, and flavors – endless!

2. Have a focus on nutrition, variety, and balance first, without calorie counting. This naturally leads to highest nutrition,

efficient digestion and gut cleansing, and full-body healing.

3. Anyone can eat like this – a meat lover, a fish fiend, vegetarians. All tastes are satisfied – the sweet tooth and the rabbit food lover, the exotic spice lover and the salt-and-pepper guy. Whether you eat at home all the time, or outside the home most of the time, you can do this. You are in control.

If there is one thing in your control, it's the food you put in your mouth. Get your act together and follow the needs of your gut, your health, and your vitality!

BEFORE YOU GO

If you liked this book you may like these other books from Lee Douglas

>>Check out more books by Lee Douglas<<

BONUS CHAPTER

Why Low Carb Diet?

Low carb diet, as the name suggests, is a diet
that is low in carbohydrates. And of course,
since the diet is low in something, it also needs
to be higher in something else. In this case,
that is the fat and protein intake. So, a diet that
is low in carbs and higher in fat and protein is
called a low carb diet. However, know that not
two low carb diet plans are the same. In fact,
there are so many different low carb meal plans
that I find it exhausting even to mention them,
let alone to choose which kind suits my needs
the best. It's no wonder why people give up
after the first roadblock. Many of these 'expert'
diets tend to have multiple phases, a lot of
restrictions, and a rather negative impact on
your gut. Starving to get the desired figure may
have short-term effects and get you in that pre-

pregnancy shirt, but it will also provide you with a lot of health issues that goes hand in hand with these kinds of diets.

 If you thought that dieting to lose weight by default means being hungry, then you are wrong, and I am glad for having the opportunity to prove you otherwise. Low carb diet shouldn't be about not eating enough, but about not enough the wrong kinds of food. And we do it all the time. Think about it, almost everything we love to consume on a daily basis has sugar in it. Why? Because sugar is addictive, and everyone knows it. So, once the food producers figured that out, that have been adding it to their products. This is why many people find it so hard to lose weight. Because the sugar is basically in every product. I am not only talking about the white refined sugar that you put in your coffee. I am talking about all of the foods that contain carbohydrates that are later broken down into unhealthy sugar during the digestion process. I am talking about those carbs that hug you around your belly and make the numbers on the scale go up. What the right low carb diet does is deprive you of these bad guys. Unlike many of the low carb diets out there that require from you to banish the carbs from your diet, even when you oh-so love them, know that this book will not give you the same guidelines. I will not ask you to completely ban the carb intake (even broccoli contains some carbohydrate, but is extremely nutritionally valuable for you). The right low carb diet bans all of the processed food from the kitchen instead and shifts your attention towards the whole foods, which is really what people have been doing since the dawn of humankind. There are many health and nutrition experts that claim how the low carb diet is just that – returning to the food that people used to consume before the processed-food era.

Just like the diet of our ancestors, the right low carb diet should mainly consist of fish, meat, eggs, and low carb fruits and vegetables.

The Benefits

It seems that the heated diet debate in which everyone seems to have taken a side is whether to choose a low carb or a low-fat diet plan. Those of you who were rooting for the 'loser' might want to change your meal plan because the evidence clearly supports the low carb diet. According to many different studies, the right low carb diet is not only a better choice because it allows you to lose significantly more weight, but also because it provides with many other health benefits.

Low Carb Diet Kills the Appetite

There is nothing worse than being hungry while dieting. If there is one thing that makes you return to your old habits and dive into a portion of cheeseburger and fries, then that is your growling tummy. Don't worry, because this diet will not leave you hungry. The best thing about this low carb diet is the fact that it actually reduces the appetite automatically. When you eat fewer carbohydrates and consume more fat and protein, you obviously get fewer calories. The trick is that this will eventually make your appetite go down, and you will end up eating even fewer calories.

Low Carb Diet has Successful Weight-Loss Results

As I said, the statistics clearly support the low carb diet. Many studies have found that, compared to other diets, the low carb diet allows the person to lose even 2-3 times more weight in the same time period. Isn't that amazing? If you are reading this book because you are looking for a way to gain your dreamy figure, then look no more.

Low Carb Diet Reduces the Blood Sugar

If you are one of the 300 million people who suffer from diabetes, you will find this news extremely helpful. It is proven that the low carb diet can decrease the blood sugar levels, improve the insulin sensitivity and bring major improvements for those suffering from type 2 diabetes. You see, after the consumption of carbohydrates, they get broken down into simple sugars (most of them are glucose) during the process of digestion. Since the blood sugar levels are toxic to the body, the body turns for help to the hormone insulin, which 'orders' the cells to burn or store the sugar. As you've already guessed, the more carbs we eat, the greater the demand for the insulin is, and that's where the problems arise. But, when you are on a low carb diet, you consume a much lower level of carbs and you significantly reduce the need for the insulin and keep your blood sugar levels in check. One study has even found that an incredible 95.2% of the participants (who were suffering from type 2 diabetes) managed to control their condition up to a point where they significantly reduced or eliminated their medications after only 6 months.

Low Carb Diet Lowers the Level of Triglycerides

Another benefit that this low carb diet can provide you with, is a lower level of triglycerides in the blood. As you know, the triglycerides are fat molecules in our blood that are elevated with a high carbohydrate consumption (mostly the fructose). Naturally, when we cut back on the carbs we also cut the triglycerides. Know that the elevated triglycerides usually cause heart diseases, so you can say that, low carb diet, also reduces the risk of developing heart diseases.

Low Carb Diet Increases the Good Cholesterol

The good cholesterol or HDL, are actually the lipoproteins that carry the cholesterol out of our body. The fat is mostly in charge of increasing the HDL levels, and since the low carb diet is high in fat, it makes the levels of the good cholesterol go up. The higher the HDL is, the lower is the risk of heart diseases. So, here is another reason how the low carb diet decreases the risk of cardiovascular diseases.

Low Carb Diet Increases the Cognitive Function

It is known that the more we eat carbohydrates and sugar, the less healthy fats we consume. This is extremely problematic for our overall health, especially because it prevents our brains from functioning properly. Many studies have found out that the intake of high glucose amounts is associated with low cognitive scores. On the other hand, a diet that is low in carbs and glucose and high in healthy fats, can improve the hormone regulation, mood control, and result in an excellent cognitive function.

Lox Carb Diet Reduces the Blood Pressure

If you struggle with hypertension, then shifting to a low carb diet is probably the best idea, since studies have shown that eating fewer carbs and more healthy fats can reduce the blood pressure significantly, which, of course, will reduce the risk of many associated diseases.

Low Carb Diet Promotes Balanced Digestion

Did you know that most of the bad bacteria in our gut thrives as a result of a high glucose intake? A diet that is high in carbs and sugar actually leads to a leaky gut syndrome and promotes the development of IBS and Candida virus. Contrary to that, the low carb diet nourishes the digestive track and prevents the bacteria from growing.

Low Carb Diet Helps Fighting Cancer

Studies have shown that a diet that is high in carbs and glucose actually feeds the cancer cells, which makes them proliferate a lot faster. By implementing a low carb diet and cutting down the glucose intake, refined carbs, and processed food, the immunity can significantly improve while the oxidative stress will decrease. That shows that the low carb diet can, in fact, act like a natural cancer treatment that may slow down the progress of the cancer cells in people affected, and reduce the risk of cancer for those that are not.

Disproving the Myths

Choose any type of diet and 'google' it, and you will come across many conflicting theories (usually all of them coming from some of the 'top experts'), and many myths wrapped around it. The low carb diet is no different. If you spend some time online and do some research on how you should plan your low carb meals, you would be surprised of the things people write. To stop the absurdity from interfering with your final goal, I have decided to reveal the truth behind some of the most common myths associated with the low carb diet.

Low Carb Means No Carb.

I really cannot wrap my head around this one, since the name itself says that it is a low carb diet, not a no-carb. However, many people believe that being on a low carb diet means eliminating the carbohydrates completely. This is, of course, not true. Even the Atkins diet, which is really, really low in carbs doesn't recommend eliminating all carbs. Although every nutritionist may have a different opinion on this diet, they all agree that some levels of carbohydrates are indeed welcome.

You Have to Count Calories to Lose Weight.

Well, maybe other diets require that you count calories and keep track of your progress that way, but not this low carb diet. While other diets may create a calorie deficit, the low carb diet alters the hormone balance and makes that deficit, organically. As I said, the low carb diet tends to cut down the appetite and make you less hungry, so, what's the point in counting calories if you eat less?

Low Carb Diet Requires a Decreased Consumption of Fruits and Vegetables.

This myth is based on the fact that most of the calories found in fruits and vegetables come from carbohydrate, and people believe that the low carb diet discourages eating veggies in fruits. Well, it is quite the opposite, actually. In fact, the food group that the low carb meal plan includes the most is the vegetable group. Non-starchy fruits and vegetables are more than allowed in the low carb meal plan; they are essential.

Low Carb Diet Is Very Restricted.

Now this is another myth. Low carb diet has only one restriction – avoid eating processed food. You can even add starchy food in your diet from time to time when you have room for it, and when your daily carb limit allows it. The only thing that is completely off the list is processed food. Everything else is allowed. The low carb diet includes a vast variety of different, whole foods.

Low Carb Diet Must Be Ketogenic.

Sorry, another myth. The ketogenic diet is a diet that is very low in carbs, and it usually includes under 50 grams of carbohydrates per day. A low carb diet, on the other hand, can be anything from 20-170 grams and perhaps even more. If you choose 150 grams of carbs to be your daily carb limit, you would be consuming a low carb diet, but not a Ketogenic one. This range will give you enough room for enjoying a starchy fruit or adding a potato to some of your meals.

Low Carb Diet Doesn't Provide All of the Nutrients.

This one must have been invented by someone who couldn't let go of the carb-loaded burrito. Just because this diet is low in carbs, doesn't mean that it is also low in nutrients. This is actually miles away from the truth since the low carb diet provides people with a lot more nutrients than what seems to be the standard Western diet, that is heavy on calories without any nutritional value. Hey, burrito man, here is something to think about next time before you dive in that large Coke?

Low Carb Diet Is Not a Long-Term Diet.

Well, let me explain this to you. Many people find the low carb diet to have pretty successful short-term results but that it isn't that successful in the long term. This is purely a myth. People usually start the low carb diet to achieve their quick weight-loss goal, so they choose a really low daily carb limit. After months of eating very restricted meals, they become tired. They achieve their goals, but after that, they usually return to their old habits and gain all of the lost weight back. It isn't the diet to blame, but their high expectations. There is nothing magical about the low carb diet. You cannot expect to lose weight quickly and to stay that way forever if you return to your junk food. That is why in this book, I recommend choosing a carb limit that you are comfortable with so that you get to receive this diet's benefits in the long haul.

If You Want Free Best Selling Kindle Books Delivered Straight To Your Inbox

JOIN OUR FREE KINDLE BOOK CLUB!

CLICK HERE

Finally, if you enjoyed this book, then I'd like to
ask you for a favor, would you be kind enough
to leave a review for this book on Amazon? It'd
be greatly appreciated!

Thank you and good luck! ☺

Lightning Source UK Ltd.
Milton Keynes UK
UKOW06f2103070617

302925UK00009B/386/P